Les aventures de Johnny L[...]
Le coq qui n'avait pa[...]

The adventures of Johnny Rabbit in

The cock that didn't crow

Nicolas Lefrançois

1

C'est **l'aube**.
Le soleil commence à se montrer
mais dans la ferme,
toute **la basse-cour** dort encore.

It is **dawn**.
The sun is rising in the sky but
all **the farmyard animals**
are still fast asleep.

Johnny, **dans son clapier**, commence seulement
à se dégourdir. Il ouvre doucement **un œil**, puis l'autre.

Johnny is just beginning to wake up **in his hutch**.
He slowly opens **one eye** and then the other.

4

- Mais ! **Le soleil** est déjà bien levé, il fait jour.
Pourquoi ne me suis-je pas réveillé ?

- Hey! **The sun** is already up and it's already day.
Why didn't I wake up before now ?

Dans la cour,
c'est l'agitation générale.
Tous les animaux
se sont rassemblés.
On s'interroge.
Pourquoi Alphonse le coq
n'a-t-il pas chanté ?
Où est-il passé ?

Everyone in the farmyard
is wondering
what is going on.
All the animals bustle
around and ask questions.
Why did Alphonse the cock
not crow ?
Where has he gone ?

6

Johnny lapin, le détective,
se dit que ce n'est pas normal.
Alphonse chante **tous les matins**
depuis des années.
Que lui est-il arrivé ?
Il a été enlevé ou alors pire,
le fermier a décidé de **le manger !**

Johnny Rabbit, the detective says to himself
that this is not right. Alphonse has been crowing
every morning for years.
What is going on ?
Somebody has taken him away or,
worse,
the farmer has decided
to **have him for dinner**.

Tout le monde se regarde **effrayé**.
Les agneaux se mettent à **pleurer**.

Everybody is looking around really **frightened**.
The lambs start **crying**.

- **Attendez**, les rassure Johnny, il est peut-être parti
faire une course ou bien il avait rendez-vous avec un ami.
- Mais il serait déjà **revenu, pleurniche** Amandine la vache.

- **Wait** a minute, Johnny says,
maybe he's gone to the shops or to meet a friend.
- Yes, but he should **be back** now,
Amandine the cow **snivels**.

Johnny décide qu'il faut **d'abord tout inspecter**.
- Essayons de **le retrouver**. Il ne peut pas être très **loin**.

Johnny decides to **make an inspection first.**
- Let's see if we can **find him.** He can't be
very **far away.**

Amandine retourne toute **la paille** dans **son étable**.

Amandine turns over all **the straw**
in **her cowshed.**

Albert, **le vieux cheval,** fouille toute **son écurie**.

Albert, **the old horse,**
is looking all around **his stable**.

Gaston, **le cochon**, nettoie **sa porcherie**.

Gaston, **the pig**, snuffles all around **his pigsty**.

Jules, **le mouton,**
inspecte **sa bergerie** avec toute sa famille.

Jules, **the sheep**, takes all his family with him
to check **his sheepfold.**

Les canards fouillent le fond de la mare.

The ducks dive down
to the bottom of **the pond** to look for him.

18

Les poules pleurent leur coq :
il n'est pas non plus dans **le poulailler**.

The hens are crying: there is no sign at all of their cock in **the henhouse.**

Johnny a bien regardé dans tous **les clapiers : rien !**

Johnny makes a careful search in all the **hutches : but nothing !**

Maintenant, c'est le tour de **la cour**.
Loupe à la patte, **rien ne peut lui échapper**.

So he decides to look around **the yard**.
Nothing could escape him when he has
his magnifying glass in his paw.

Soudain, il entend un **sifflement étrange** près du gros **tas de fumier**.

Suddenly, he hears a **whistling sound** near the big **heap of manure**.

Il s'approche et se met à **renifler**.
- **Pouah ! Ça sent vraiment très mauvais !**

He goes up close to it and starts **sniffling.**
- **Yuck ! That really stinks !**

Pas d'autre solution, il faut s'y engouffrer.
- **Mais**, ce n'est pas un sifflement, c'est **un petit ronflement**.
Qui peut bien s'endormir dans **le fumier** ?

But there is **no other solution**,
he has to check out this noise.
- **Hey,** that's not whistling, that's **snoring**.
Who on earth is sleeping in **the manure heap** ?

- Vous m'avez réveillé,
répond une voix toute ensommeillée et fâchée.
- **Ça y est, j'ai retrouvé Alphonse**, crie Johnny.

- You woke me up,
a voice says, very sleepy and very annoyed too.
- **Hey, I've found Alphonse,** shouts Johnny.

La basse-cour **se rassemble** au grand complet,
ravie que son coq préféré soit retrouvé.
- Hip, hip hourra, pour Johnny !

All the farmyard animals **gather around,**
delighted that Alphonse the cock has been found.
- **Hip, hip hooray for Johnny !**

Alphonse doit maintenant **s'expliquer.**
- Pour une fois, je voulais faire **la grasse matinée**
sans être dérangé.
Je me suis donc **caché** là
où on ne viendrait pas me chercher.

Vous ne pouviez pas me laisser
tranquille ?

Alphonse has now **to explain** everything.
- You see, I wanted to have **a good long sleep**
for once without being disturbed.
So I **hid** here where nobody
would come looking for me.

Couldn't you all
just **leave me in peace ?**

- Nous nous sommes tous **inquiétés**, s'écrie Gaston.

- We were all so **worried** about you, squeals Gaston.

- Tu nous as fait **peur**, pleurnichent les poules rassurées.
Mais nous sommes bien **contentes**
qu'il ne te soit rien arrivé.
Viens avec nous, nous allons te nettoyer.

- You gave us a **fright**, cackled all the hens
together. But now we're **happy** that nothing
has happened to you.
Come along with us, we'll clean all that yucky
stuff off you.

Une fois de plus,
Johnny, le détective de la ferme, peut être **satisfait.**
Il a résolu **l'énigme**
du coq qui n'avait pas chanté !

Once again,
Johnny, the farm detective,
can be **pleased** with his work.
He has solved **the mystery**
of the cock that didn't crow !

Les animaux et leurs petits. **The animals and their young.**

Le petit de la brebis s'appelle...
The ewe's baby is called a lamb.

Le petit de la vache s'appelle...
The cow's baby is called a calf.

Le petit de la cane s'appelle...
The duck's baby is called a duckling.

Le petit de la jument s'appelle...

The mare's baby is called a foal.

Le petit de la poule s'appelle...

The hen's baby is called a chick.

Le petit de la truie s'appelle...

The sow's baby is called a piglet.

Où habitent-ils ?
Where do they live ?

L'écurie.
The stable.

La mare.
The pond.

La vache.
The cow.

La porcherie.
The pigsty.

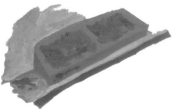

La poule.
The hen.

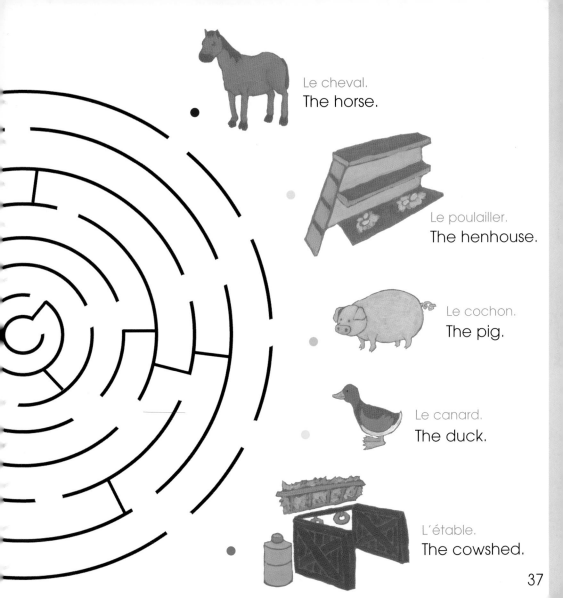

Le cheval.
The horse.

Le poulailler.
The henhouse.

Le cochon.
The pig.

Le canard.
The duck.

L'étable.
The cowshed.

37

Vocabulaire : Vocabulary

a	l'agneau	=	the lamb
	l'ami	=	the friend
	l'animal	=	the animal
	l'aube	=	the dawn
b	la basse-cour	=	the farmyard
	la bergerie	=	the sheepfold
c	se cacher	=	to hide
	le canard	=	the duck
	chanter	=	to sing
	le cheval	=	the horse
	le clapier	=	the hutch
	le cochon	=	the pig
	le coq	=	the cock
	crier	=	to shout
e	l'écurie	=	the stable
	l'énigme	=	the mystery
	l'étable	=	the cowshed
f	la famille	=	the family
	la ferme	=	the farm
	le fermier	=	the farmer
i	s'inquiéter	=	to worry

	inspecter	=	to inspect
	s'interroger	=	to wonder
j	le jour	=	the day
l	la loupe	=	the magnifying glass
m	manger	=	to eat
	la mare	=	the pond
	le mouton	=	the sheep
o	l'oeil	=	the eye
p	la paille	=	the straw
	la patte	=	the paw
	pleurer	=	to cry
	la porcherie	=	the pigsty
	le poulailler	=	the henhouse
	la poule	=	the hen
r	se rassembler	=	to gather
	renifler	=	to sniff
	retrouver	=	to find
	se réveiller	=	to wake up
s	le sifflement	=	the whistling
	le soleil	=	the sun
v	la vache	=	the cow
	la voix	=	the voice

Conjugaison du verbe **auxiliaire** **être : to be**

présent	**simple present**
je suis	I am
tu es	you are
il/elle est	he/she/it is
nous sommes	we are
vous êtes	you are
ils/elles sont	they are

passé composé	**simple present perfect**
j'ai été	I have been
tu as été	you have been
il/elle a été	he/she/it has been
nous avons été	we have been
vous avez été	you have been
ils/elles ont été	they have been

imparfait	**simple preterite**
j'étais	I was
tu étais	you were
il/elle était	he/she/it was
nous étions	we were
vous étiez	you were
ils/elles étaient	they were

passé simple
je fus
tu fus
il fut
nous fûmes
vous fûtes
ils/elles furent

simple preterite

futur
je serai
tu seras
il/elle sera
nous serons
vous serez
ils/elles seront

future
I will be
you will be
he/she/it will be
we will be
you will be
they will be

Remarque importante :

les temps de conjugaison anglais ne correspondent pas
exactement aux temps français.
Notre juxtaposition ne tient pas compte des nombreuses nuances
et ne donne donc qu'une idée relative de l'emploi réel
des temps anglais afin de pouvoir se référer au texte.

Conjugaison du verbe **auxiliaire** **avoir : to have**

présent

j'ai
tu as
il/elle a
nous avons
vous avez
ils/elles ont

simple present

I have
you have
he/she/it has
we have
you have
they have

passé composé

j'ai eu
tu as eu
il/elle a eu
nous avons eu
vous avez eu
ils/elles ont eu

simple present perfect

I have had
you have had
he/she/it has had
we have had
you have had
they have had

imparfait

j'avais
tu avais
il/elle avait
nous avions
vous aviez
ils/elles avaient

simple preterite

I had
you had
he/she/it had
we had
you had
they had

passé simple

j' eus
tu eus
il eut
nous eûmes
vous eûtes
ils/elles eurent

futur

j'aurai
tu auras
il/elle aura
nous aurons
vous aurez
ils/elles auront

simple preterite

future

I will have
you will have
he/she/it will have
we will have
you will have
they will have

Conjugaison des **verbes réguliers** comme :

to cry, to worry.

simple present : I cry
he/she/it cries
we/you/they cry

simple present perfect: I have cried
he/she/it has cried
we/you/they have cried

simple preterite : I cried
he/she/it cried
we/you/they cried

future : I will cry
he/she/it will cry
we/you/they will cry

Conjugaison des verbes **irréguliers.**

Les verbes irréguliers se conjuguent comme les verbes
réguliers mais leur forme change au prétérit
et au participe passé.

	infinitif	prétérit	participe passé
to eat	eat	ate	eaten
			(ex: I have eaten)
to find	find	found	found
			(ex: they have found)
to hide	hide	hid	hidden
			(ex: we have hidden)

Notes :

Notes :